TEATIME WITH MRS. GRAMMAR PERSON

BARBARA VENKATARAMAN

CONTENTS

BOOKS BY BARBARA VENKATARAMAN

Death by Didgeridoo (Jamie Quinn Cozy Mystery #1)

The Case of the Killer Divorce (Jamie Quinn Cozy Mystery #2)

Peril in the Park (Jamie Quinn Cozy Mystery #3)

Engaged in Danger (Jamie Quinn Cozy Mystery #4)

Jeopardy in July (Jamie Quinn Cozy Mystery #5)

Malice in Miami (Jamie Quinn Cozy Mystery #6)

Jamie Quinn Mysteries Box Set: Books 1-3

Jamie Quinn Mysteries Box Set: Books 4-6

Jamie Quinn Mysteries Box Set: Books 1-6

I'm Not Talking About You, Of Course (Quirky Essays for Quirky People #1)

A Trip to the Hardware Store (Quirky Essays for Quirky People #2)

A Smidge of Crazy (Quirky Essays for Quirky People #3)

Teatime with Mrs. Grammar Person

If You'd Just Listened To Me In The First Place

The Fight for Magicallus

Accidental Activist: Justice for the Groveland Four (Co-Author)

Scary Shorts: Flash Fiction

Holiday Shorts: Flash Fiction

Valentine Shorts: Flash Fiction

Dog Days of Summer Shorts: Flash Fiction
A Year of Shorts: Flash Fiction

MRS. GRAMMAR PERSON

FEAR NOT, GENTLE WRITER, FOR HELP HAS arrived. Rest assured that your grimaces and groans, your grinding of teeth have not gone unnoticed. And, because Mrs. Grammar Person abhors the grinding of perfectly good teeth, she has agreed to impart her timely wisdom to those afflicted with self-doubt.

In a stage whisper Mrs. Grammar Person explains that although she is your true friend, spell-check is not. Spell-check is fickle and delights in trickery. He will make you believe that it's *morning* when, in fact, you're *in mourning*, or that you should *waver* when you are seeking a *waiver*. He doesn't care if your simple *please* turns into multiple *pleas*, and he will most likely *desert* you if you ask for *dessert*.

Mrs. G.P. wishes to remind you for whom the bell tolls (if you must ask, it tolls for thee). When in doubt as to whether to use who or whom, simply substitute the word *him*. If *him* will do nicely then the word you want is *whom*. Mrs. G.P. shudders to think that you would even consider writing "For *he* the bell tolls." She keeps her smelling salts handy, just in case.

Being an agreeable person herself Mrs. G.P. insists that all of her nouns and verbs also agree; therefore, a *swarm of bees* searches for honey but the *two straggler bees* search on their own. How sweet the sound of proper grammar!

While Mrs. G.P. has nothing but admiration for writers who seek perfection, she cautions that nobody is perfect (except for her, of course). To that end, she cautions you about using the pronoun "I" when the word you seek is "me". To write that "the teacher allows Joe and I to go to the playground" is tantamount to writing, "the teacher allows "I" to go to the playground." Whenever she sees this transgression Mrs. G.P. slams the offending book shut, never to be opened again.

Now it is time to bid farewell to Mrs. Grammar Person but before she takes her leave she asks you to remember that: it is always darkest before the dawn, when the going gets tough, the tough get going, you should always keep your chin up and, if you don't stop using clichés, Mrs. Grammar Person will march back here and rap your knuckles with a ruler!

Once she is satisfied that you've learned your lesson, Mrs. G.P. gently pats you on the head and heads off to the library, casually tossing out her final words of wisdom, words that shake your very foundation: "Remember, my dears, you *can* end a sentence with a preposition and you *can* split an infinitive!"

FEAR NOT, GENTLE WRITER, MRS. GRAMMAR Person, heeding your cry for help, has returned, delighted to be of service once again. Like you Mrs. G.P revels in the knowledge that, while fashions may come and go (both the tasteful and the tacky), exceptional grammar never goes out of style. It is her fervent hope that her words of wisdom serve to *complement* your knowledge so that you receive nothing but *compliments* in your writing.

Mrs. G.P. marvels at the difference a single letter can make! She knows that the *effect* of her words deeply *affect* you. Especially once you come to realize that *effect* is a noun and *affect* is a verb (This is the most common usage, dear ones. *Affect* can also be a noun when used to signify *demeanor*. *Effect* can also be a verb when used to mean *to bring about* or *to accomplish*.)

She *brings* you these tidbits so that you may *take* them with you, safely ensconced in your heart, along with your affection for your favorite grammarian. Coyly, Mrs. Grammar Person reminds you that you *bring* things toward you, but *take* things away from you.

Mrs. G. P. wants you to know that you can always count on her. And speaking of counting, here is a handy rule: when using "fewer" or "less" in a sentence, if you can count it, use the word "fewer", if you cannot, use the word "less". Another excellent rule to live by is this one: Less is more. Nobody likes to hear anything twice, so it's best to avoid being repetitious, redundant, reiterative, and duplicative in your writing, dear ones. As Shakespeare taught us, brevity is the soul of wit!

When Mrs. Grammar Person hears of the mistakes her writers frequently make, she feels an attack of the vapors coming on and must immediately lie down. She lays her head on the pillow and waits for her devotees to understand the difference between *lie* and *lay*. *Lay* must always have an object. Thus, you *lay* the book on the counter but *lie* down. One way to remember this is to tell yourself that people lie, but Mrs. G. P. disagrees, believing that most people are honest and good.

Mrs. Grammar Person has enjoyed chatting with you today and hopes that you follow her advice, not out of admiration for her, but because of its own intrinsic worth. Mrs. G. P. will sleep well tonight knowing that you understand "it's" is a contraction of it and is while "its" is the possessive form and requires no apostrophe. Ever.

Mrs. Grammar Person fondly bids you adieu, Gentle Writers, comforted by the thought that your paths will cross again.

MRS. GRAMMAR PERSON AND THE GENTLEMAN CALLER

Fear not, Gentle Writer, Mrs. Grammar Person would not abandon you in your hour of need-- not when you face potential pitfalls at every turn: an avalanche of apostrophes, a mountain of misplaced modifiers, and a desert of dangling participles. The horror! In truth, Mrs. G. P. *gets* it but fervently hopes that "get" is a word you choose to forget. Excellent writing, (the only kind that merits discussion) has no place for such a silly word, a word tossed about hither and yon, a word which is the first and last resort of a lazy lay-about. When Mrs. G.P. reads that it's time to "get going", or for people to "get to know each other", she feels quite faint. Once she has recovered (with the help of a strong pot of tea and some lovely biscuits), she firmly replaces the offending word with a proper verb.

While our favorite grammarian is deciding which topic to embark upon next (there are so many, after all), she hears a knock at the door. Delighted by the thought of an unexpected guest Mrs. G.P. perks up and answers the door. An older gentleman looking very dapper in a morning suit and top hat greets Mrs. G.P. with a shy smile.

"Please pardon the intrusion, dear lady, but having read your blog posts, I feel that you are a kindred spirit and wish to make your acquaintance."

Although accustomed to the admiration of her devotees Mrs. G.P. is nonetheless humbled and flattered by the attention.

"Do tell," she replies, giving him an arch look before inviting him into her office. "Clearly, only an Englishman such as yourself could appreciate the beauty of our shared language."

With a flourish the gentleman tips his hat to Mrs. Grammar Person before removing it. "I hope you don't think it impolite that I've come to take a *peek* at you, but your writing has *piqued* my interest. In fact, I am at the *peak* of my curiosity."

Mrs. G.P. claps her hands with amusement. "Bravo! Well done! How clever of you. That someone so *discreet* can comprehend such *discrete* possibilities; it's wonderful."

Beaming at her the guest nods in agreement. "And how fascinating that both words derive from the same Latin word, *discretus,* which means separated. Don't you agree?"

Of course Mrs. Grammar Person agrees--how could she not, when she carefully analyzes the origin of each word she encounters? For example, *continuously* means continuing uninterrupted while *continually* means continuing over a long period of time with interruption. So interesting!

"*May* I beg your indulgence?" asks the esteemed gentleman, lightly kissing the hand of the startled

Mrs. G.P. "Although I fear I *might've* gone too far already..."

Our favorite grammarian quickly recovers her composure and makes a confession to her befuddled guest. "One *prays* to hear high *praise*, yet it *preys* upon one's mind to desire it too much."

The gentleman chuckles. "At the risk of exaggerating to the point of hyperbole I must say, Mrs. Grammar Person, you are the jewel in the crown. I feel I have overstayed my welcome and will take my leave now. I hope to visit you again. I would consider it the highest honor." He tips his hat and turns to go.

Mrs. G.P. sees him to the door. "But I never asked your name, sir, how terribly rude of me."

Cheerfully, he replies, "My name is Mr. Syntax and it was a pleasure to make your acquaintance."

With a knowing smile Mrs. GP nods. "I sense that we will become fast friends indeed!"

MRS. GRAMMAR PERSON WISHES YOU GOOD CHEER

FEAR NOT, GENTLE WRITER, MRS. GRAMMAR Person would not abandon you to your own devices simply because the holidays are upon us. To the contrary, it is at this time of year that Mrs. G.P. frets the most about her devoted fans. During this, the gift-giving season, you must remember that, try as you might, you will never find the most unique gift for that special someone. *Unique* means one-of-a-kind; therefore, one gift cannot be more or less unique than any other. But, whichever gift you choose, Mrs. G.P. is sure that you will delight the recipient!

In addition to gifts the holidays provide us with bountiful treats. *Everybody* loves these treats and *nobody* can pass them up. Mrs. G. P. finds it curious that the word *everybody* is followed by a singular verb despite that it refers to many people. Nevertheless, she diligently follows all of the rules of grammar, even the silly ones. Likewise, it is correct to say: *all of them* enjoyed *their* cookies, but *each* boy enjoyed *his* cookie. Our favorite grammarian is proud of her ability to *home* in on these grammatical mishaps, but she cannot *hone* in on them, since that makes no sense at all.

To clarify, Mrs. Grammar Person would not *imply* that you make such egregious errors and prays that you have not *inferred* as much from her writings. She is confident that you would never confuse the meanings of *imply* and *infer*. Mrs. G.P. knows that you follow her musings out of a mutual love for perfect grammar and that you *lend* her your attention willingly. Of course, you couldn't *loan* her your attention because *loan* is a noun and *lend* is a verb. But you already knew that. Like Mrs. Grammar Person, you are an expert grammarian who advises others of the logic (and sometimes illogic) of proper English. Whether they choose to take your advice is up to them. Isn't it a marvel how one letter can change the meaning of a word? An airplane *hangar* transforms into a simple clothes *hanger*, an apple *peel* becomes the *peal* of a bell, and the act of being *stationary* in one place becomes *stationery* for letter-writing. Mrs. G.P. cannot discuss the difference between *naval* and *navel* because it always gives her a fit of the giggles to compare the Navy to a belly button.

Once the holidays are over we strengthen our resolve to eat properly and exercise after the over-indulgence we have all succumbed to. Mrs. G.P reminds us that we should also endeavor to strengthen our writing and eliminate the passive tense whenever possible. Thus, instead of saying "The cookies were eaten by the boys", you should say "The boys ate the cookies." Whose cookies are we discussing? The boys' cookies, of course. The apostrophe indicates the possessive (the cookies belong to the boys) and the apostrophe follows the 's' because the cookies belong to all of the them. Were Mrs. G.P. to speak of a single boy and his cookies she would write, "the boy's cookies".

This leads Mrs. Grammar Person to answer a final question that she has been asked recently, to wit, "what gift would she like to receive?" Feeling humbled our beloved grammarian hesitates, deep in thought. Finally, she responds that she would like a "grammar-repair kit", a toolbox filled with apostrophes, hyphens, and an endless supply of White-Out so that she may fix the mistakes she encounters daily. But the gift she wants most of all, she adds with a smile, is the gift of your continued friendship throughout next year and beyond. A happy holiday to all of you, my dear grammarians!

MRS. GRAMMAR PERSON
HELPS OUT

FEAR NOT, GENTLE WRITER, MRS. GRAMMAR Person has heard your pleas and is happy to be of assistance--just as soon as she finishes her cup of tea. Ah, much better! Of course, Mrs. G.P. would not be able to *hear* your plaintive cry nor *assist* you in any way were it not for the existence of verbs, yes, those versatile words that allow us to take action. Without them, we couldn't budge at all.

Helping out is something Mrs. G.P. adores, which is why she holds a special place in her heart for the helping verbs. *Helping verbs* can stand on their own, certainly, but they are also kind enough to help out the other verbs. Below is a list of the helping verbs and, should you choose to memorize these verbs as Mrs. G.P. has done, you will *never* forget them. Even if you cannot for the life of you remember something extremely important, you will always remember the helping verbs. You may wish to take heed of this friendly advice from your favorite grammarian. Now that you have been warned, here is a complete list of the *helping verbs*:

am, is, are, was, were, be, being, been, have, has,

had, do, does, did, can, could, shall, should, will, would, may, might, must.

Whew! Mrs. Grammar Person loves to recite this list as fast as she can; it is one of her daily grammar exercises. An example of a helping verb *can be found* in the short sentence: "I am going." How silly of Mrs. G.P. not to notice *another* example of a helping verb in the previous phrase "**can be** found"! She can't wait to tell that story at the annual Grammar convention.

Now that you have mastered the helping verbs (and Mrs. G.P. has refilled her teapot), it is time to discuss the trickier verbs, the ones that defy logic, the ones that follow their own rules. Yes, as unpleasant as it may be, we must examine the *irregular verbs.* To ease you into this topic, our beloved grammarian starts with the easy ones. These verbs are irregular in that they stay the same, no matter what happens. In an ever-changing world, you can always count on these verbs to hold their course. Thus, if Mrs. G.P. were to *let* you down (which she hopes will never happen), then *let* remains the same whether she let you down today, she let you down yesterday, or she has let you down in the past (past participle). These verbs are your constant friends and include the words: *bet, bid, cost, hit, hurt, let, cut, broadcast, put,* and *shut.* Another verb in this category is the word *read,* which keeps the same spelling, but changes pronunciation from present to past tense.

The next group of verbs is only a little tricky in that they change form from present to past, but remain the same for past participle. An example is: "Mrs. G.P. *holds* your friendship dear; she *held* it dear yesterday, as she *has held* it dear always.

There are many verbs that follow this rule; some examples are:

beat/beat/beaten
catch/caught/caught
hang/hung/hung
lay/laid/laid

Finally, Mrs. G.P. hopes that you have remained true in your devotion to grammar and are prepared to tackle the most irregular of irregular verbs. As she cannot explain their oddness away, Mrs. Grammar Person will simply list some of them for your future reference:

Awake/awoke/awoken (This verb causes a lot of confusion, indeed!)

Be/was/been ("To be or not to be" *was* the question that *had been* on Hamlet's mind)

Become/became/become (That's a strange one)

Begin/began/begun (I *begin* to see why you *began* the war you should never have *begun*)

Bite/bit/bitten (I *bite* the boy who *bit* me first and now we *have bitten* each other)

Blow/blew/blown (The wind *blows* as much as it *blew* yesterday, but not as much as it *has blown* in the past)

Break/broke/broken (I *break* a different toe than I *broke* yesterday, but the same one I *have broken* before)

There are many others which may easily be found online for your edification and enlightenment:

As much as she lives for the rules of grammar, Mrs. G.P. must admit that she is a tad weary after her foray into the land of irregular verbs. She wishes to take a nap and, being a creature of habit, will *lie* down in the same place she *lay* yesterday and *has lain* whenever she feels the need for respite--the Queen Anne sofa in her drawing room. After all of your hard work, Gentle Writer, you should rest as well. Mrs. G.P. bids you a fond farewell until the next time you meet.

MRS. GRAMMAR PERSON IS MELANCHOLY

Fear not, Gentle Writer, Mrs. Grammar Person will not fill your head with verbs today for she is filled with melancholy. Having heard dreadful news of a dear friend's illness Mrs. G.P. feels despondent. Not even a pot of tea and a visit from her favorite cat, Mr. Malaprop, has served to lift her from the doldrums. And so she turns to you, her admirers and, dare we say, friends, in her hour of need because chatting with you always makes her smile.

Why yes, Mrs. G.P. would be glad to explain the origin of her cat's name--and she thanks you for the distraction. A *malapropism* is a funny thing indeed and is defined as a misused word or a verbal slip. An example is "he put out the flames with a fire distinguisher". Mrs. G.P. recalls an amusing malapropism from a young child who, after seeing a commercial about lactose intolerance, declared that he, too, was "black toast intolerant". Another interesting word ending in -ism is *solipsism*, which means egotistical self-absorption. Mrs. Grammar Person shudders to think that this term would ever be used to describe her.

To lighten the mood and banish dark thoughts our favorite grammarian would like to tell you about *spoonerisms*, words in which some of the parts are switched, either through error or wordplay, with humorous results. Named after the Reverend William Archibald Spooner, who was famous for these gaffes, an example of a spoonerism can be found in this question he once posed, "Is it kisstomary to cuss the bride?" Unlike other men of the cloth who focused on *proselytism* (converting others to your religion or way of thinking), this good reverend could not be taken seriously.

On the subject of being taken seriously a true grammarian would do well to avoid *anachronisms* in his writing. From the Greek root word khrono, an anachronism is something or someone that is out of chronological order. Thus, were you to write about Colonial times you would not include a reference to television--unless, of course, your story involved time travel.

Another serious topic is *plagiarism*. When Mrs. G.P. was a girl her mother warned her to never lie for she would always be caught. The same can be said about plagiarism. But do not despair, your beloved grammarian is sympathetic and understands that with so many ideas whirling about your brain it is difficult to distinguish which are original and which are borrowed. Enter the internet, a 'place' where any phrase may be tested for originality. By using this safeguard you may rest assured that your *witticisms, symbolism, epigrammatism,* and *lyricism* will always be your own creation and that you will never be accused of *charlatanism*. To express that in simpler terms, don't be a Luddite.

With a sense of *absurdism* Mrs. G.P. reports that there are 887 words that end with -ism, including the word *ism*. But, unlike Don Quixote, your beloved grammarian will not fall prey to *quixotism* (being caught up in the romance of noble deeds and the pursuit of unreachable goals) and attempt to discuss all 887. That would be a terrible example of *didacticism* on her part! Instead, Mrs. Grammar Person will dispense with her *defeatism* and *pessimism*, at least for today, and focus on the *spiritualism* and *humanism* of her followers and friends and thank them for their *altruism* in lifting her spirits. Until the next time, your favorite grammarian sends you gratitude and affection.

MRS. GRAMMAR PERSON IS AMUSED

Fear not, Gentle Writer, Mrs. Grammar Person is out of the doldrums and no longer feels dull, listless, or in low spirits. The word "doldrums", from the Old English word *dol,* means foolish or dull, but you may rest assured that Mrs. G.P. would never think you were foolish for feeling dull. No, she would try to raise your spirits in the same way she raises her own--with the most delightfully entertaining words imaginable.

Mrs. G.P. is sensing a scintilla of sympathy and an iota of interest from you, her devoted admirers, so she will explain her method *lickety split.* She will not *shilly shally* (procrastinate) or *dilly dally* (delay) or *lollygag* (dawdle) another minute, although she doesn't wish to proceed in a way that's *willy nilly* (disorganized) or *pell mell* (in a recklessly hurried manner). Nor does she wish to start a *brouhaha* (an uproar) or, worse, a *hullaballoo* (condition of noisy confusion). Mrs. G.P. fears that all of this *jibber jabber* (talk in a rapid and excited way that is difficult to understand) could give you a case of *tintinnabulation* (the sound of ringing), or worse, a headache. She would not want to leave you *befuddled* (confused) or *flummoxed* (bewildered) because of too much *gobbledygook* (meaningless or nonsensical language). On the other hand, Mrs. Grammar Person does not believe in *mollycoddling* anyone; she believes that would be *feckless* (irresponsible) of her and cause some *scuttlebutt* (gossip, rumors) among her fellow grammarians, some of whom (Mrs. G.P. hates to say it) tend to *bloviate* (speak pompously or brag).

Far be it from Mrs. Grammar Person to pull any *shenanigans* (foolish behavior) or engage in any form of *skullduggery* (deception or trickery). Au contraire! She simply wants you to enjoy the same *mellifluous* (sweet-sounding) words she does, laughing at how silly some of them sound. As Mrs. Grammar Person sits by her pond pondering the *pollywogs* (which she refuses to call tadpoles) her mind drifts and she wonders whether a rose by any other name would really smell as sweet. She leaves that to you to decide, for it is late and Mrs. G.P. must *skedaddle* (hurry off) as she has a dinner engagement with her new friend, Mr. Syntax. Until the next time, Mrs. Grammar Person bids you adieu!

MRS. GRAMMAR PERSON MAKES A TOAST

FEAR NOT, GENTLE WRITER, MRS. GRAMMAR Person will not abandon you despite the fact that it is the busiest time of year and she hasn't finished making her cookies. Nay, Mrs. G.P. knows that if grammarians don't remain vigilant and make every effort to ensure clear communication, then civilization will surely fall. And, while many civilized people prefer to use the word *insure* instead of *ensure*, Mrs. G.P. *assures* us that *ensure* is preferable unless, of course, you sell insurance.

As it is the season for childlike wonder Mrs. G.P. stops to wonder why *childlike* connotes a return to happier times while *childish* is an insult used for adults who embody the worst aspects of childhood, such as whining, tattling, or tantrums. This is indeed a mystery, one that we don't have the *capability* to solve although we surely have the *ability* to use both words correctly. The words ability and capability are often used interchangeably, but are not the same. *Capability* usually means extremes of ability or potential ability, while *ability* refers to a current level of achievement or skill. Likewise, the word *capacity* may refer to a talent one was born with, while *ability* is a skill one must learn. Isn't it *addictive* to learn the nuances of grammar and word usage? Some would say it's *addicting,* and although Mrs. G.P. would applaud the sentiment she would disagree with the word choice.

Not wanting to start an argument our favorite grammarian would *defuse* the situation by offering the person one of her *addictive* home-baked delicacies. Her only wish is for good grammar to be *diffused* across the land but if she cannot have good grammar, she will settle for good cheer, especially during holiday time.

Speaking of time, Mrs. Grammar Person always spends *some time* answering e-mails from her devoted fans, as well as those from *sometime* grammarians, whom she refers to as dabblers. It has been *some time* since Mrs. G.P. received such an e-mail, but it did happen again *sometime* yesterday. This particular dabbler proclaimed there to be no difference between the words, *everyday* and *every day* and challenged Mrs. G.P. to prove otherwise. Always up to a challenge our favorite phonetic-fanatic rolled up her metaphorical sleeves and wrote:

My dear Sir,

It is not an *everyday* (ordinary, daily) occurrence for me to receive a request such as yours. If it happened *every day*, then I would have no time for my baking. *Everyday* is an adjective, while *every day* is an adjective followed by a noun. Whenever you are unsure as to which form to use, may I suggest that you substitute each day and, if that makes sense, then *every day* is the correct choice.

All the best,
Mrs. Grammar Person

As you might imagine, Mrs. G.P. has heard nothing *further* from him, not even a thank-you, but, no matter, she has much to prepare and her mind wanders *farther* from the rules of grammar than she would care to admit. She must choose *between* baking and wrapping gifts, but since decisiveness is *among* her many talents, she bustles off to wrap gifts. To her consternation, she notes that the pajamas she bought for her niece are marked *inflammable* but that the incense she bought for her yogi is marked *flammable*. What unnecessary confusion! To clarify, Mrs. G.P. writes identical cards to attach to the packages. The cards make it clear that each gift will catch fire quite easily.

Exhausted from so much activity, Mrs. Grammar Person sinks into an overstuffed chaise lounge in her drawing room. Her furniture is a soothing rose color because chintz makes her dizzy. She is startled to hear the doorbell ring and, flustered, she rushes to answer it. Who is it, but her new friend, Mr. Syntax, holding a bottle of champagne wrapped with a bow. With a broad smile and a happy glow, our favorite grammarian invites him in.

"I hope that you'll pardon the intrusion," the gentleman says, shyly. "But I was in the neighborhood and wanted to bring you a holiday gift. Something as bubbly as you are."

Mrs. G.P. notices that this is no ordinary champagne, but, in fact, the most expensive French variety. She hesitates to take the bottle.

"But, Mr. Syntax, I cannot accept something so *valuable*. It's too much..."

Looking crestfallen Mr. Syntax replies, "Mrs. G.P., I consider your friendship *invaluable* (priceless beyond measure) and this is but a token of my appreciation." He looks so sad that even his moustache droops.

Our favorite grammarian has an idea. "I cannot accept this expensive gift, but I am happy to drink it with you."

"Brilliant!" he replies, bouncing back to his old self. He pops the cork while she fetches the champagne flutes.

They sit next to each other in front of the fire crackling on the hearth.

"To a beautiful friendship!" says Mr. Syntax, raising his glass.

"To a wonderful new friend!" says Mrs. Grammar Person. Glasses clink and delicate champagne bubbles float away, right into the New Year.

Fear not, Gentle Writer, for Mrs. Grammar Person, hearing your sighs and seeing your furrowed brows, is delighted to offer her assistance once again. She knows the source of your consternation, the impetus for your aggravation; more absurd than an irregular verb is the mixed-up sound of an irregular noun. When *mouse* becomes *mice* and *louse* becomes *lice*--it's truly enough to make you think twice. These three nouns are also offbeat: *tooth* becomes *teeth*, *goose* becomes *geese* and *foot* becomes *feet*.

But some nouns don't change, and that is just fine, for no matter how many, a *swine* is a *swine*. Other animal nouns that are equally clear are *moose*, *sheep* and *fish*, *bison*, *tuna* and *deer*. Alas, Mrs. G.P. cannot grant all your wishes, for sometimes *fish* can also be *fishes*.

Before spending time berating ourselves, we must figure out how *elf* became *elves*. Some nouns ending with 'f' change into 'v', so Henry VIII had six *wives*, do you see? Each *wife* had a *scarf*, six *scarves* did they have, worn around their necks and not on their *calves*.

I cut food with a *knife*, though I own many *knives*, a dog has one *life*, while a cat has nine *lives*. I buy bread by the *loaf*, I can't eat many *loaves*, but two or more *oafs* will never be *oaves*. *Fluff* and *stuff* never change, thank heavens for that, like a dog is a dog, but never a cat.

The next three nouns are really quite mild, and clearly address each *man*, *woman*, and *child*. *Men*, *women*, and *children* is the rule you must ken, to understand that the plural of *ox* is *oxen*.

The next three are tricky--stick with it, please--or you'll never understand *appendices*. With *appendix*, *index*, and *matrix*, you'd never guess, but the plural of each ends with "c-e-s".

The next nouns are Latin and make quite a fuss, and include such strange words as *nucleus*. Mrs. G.P. regrets very much that she might make you cry, but the plural of *nucleus* is *nuclei*. Please *focus* your mind and you'll learn by and by, that the plural of *focus* is always *foci*. A *cactus* can blind you if you're poked in the eye, for nothing hurts more than sharpened *cacti*. A mushroom's a *fungus* and healthy to try, but more than one type is known as *fungi*. Yes, your head hurts, we know--too many *stimuli*.

More Latin for you, these nouns are more rare, the plural's the form that gives them their flair. Mrs. G.P. hopes she won't make you feel dumb when she tells you that *data* are composed of *datum* (*media/medium*, *bacteria/bacterium*). Likewise, *criteria* means more than one, but the singular form is *criterion*.

Our *crisis* averted, no more *crises* today, Mrs. G.P.'s *diagnosis* is that you'll be okay. Her *analysis* complete, she finishes up with a flourish, and hopes that her rhymes weren't too amateurish. Changing *person* to *people* is our final odd duck and now Mrs. Grammar Person has run out of luck. You're happy to leave her for nothing is worse, than listening to Mrs. G.P. composing in verse!

MRS. GRAMMAR PERSON'S
WISHFUL THINKING

Fear not, Gentle Writer, Mrs. Grammar Person is here--and it seems that she has arrived just in time! The sight of you pulling your hair out and chewing your nails makes her sorry she didn't arrive sooner. But, no need to fret, Mrs. G.P can see what the problem is and although she *wishes* there *were a* simple solution, alas, there is not. The truth is that the *subjunctive tense* is tricky and so, before she can begin to explain it, our favorite grammarian will need a strong pot of tea and some lovely biscuits. If you are in the neighborhood, you're welcome to join her for tea; she always buys extra biscuits, just in case.

Ah, much better! Now, Mrs. G.P. is ready to discuss the tense which makes everyone tense, the strange and wonderful, wonderfully strange subjunctive tense, the tense that allows us to engage in wishful thinking, to imagine things as they might have been, and to impose our will on others *as if we were royalty*, which, happily, we are not--that's why we had to use the subjunctive.

We may not be royalty, Mrs. Grammar Person says, but we can still impose our will on others by *in-*

sisting, demanding, commanding, urging, proposing, requesting, suggesting, asking, advising, recommending, and *desiring* that they take a particular action. Before you beg off with a migraine, please allow Mrs. G.P. to explain that the subjunctive tense often looks identical to the indicative tense--depending on whom you are bossing around. For example, "They *walk* to the park" is indicative. "I *insist that* they *walk* to the park" is subjunctive, but *walk* is still *walk*. So, why all the fuss? The fuss comes about when the speaker imposes his will on *him* or *her* (and sometimes *them*). Let's try it again see what happens. "He *walks* to the park" is indicative. "I demand that he *walk* to the park" is subjunctive. We see how the verb has changed, don't we?

Other ways we can impose our will on others (thereby requiring the use of the subjunctive) is with the following expressions:

It is important (that)
It is recommended (that)
It is urgent (that)
It is vital (that)
It is a good idea (that)
It is a bad idea (that)
It is best (that)
It is crucial (that)
It is desirable (that)
It is essential (that)
It is imperative (that)

Sometimes we are feeling more hopeful than willful, but even when we wish or hope for something to occur, we must still use the subjunctive. "I *wish* my brother *weren't* so stubborn" is wishful thinking because the speaker's brother is clearly stubborn and seems unlikely to change.

The subjunctive is used to describe conditions that are not true, as well as for commands, wishes, and requests. Most commonly, the subjunctive is used to describe a hypothetical situation that isn't likely to happen, such as, "*If* she *were* any tinier, she would be an ant." A factual statement would be: "*When* she *was* very tiny, she was just a baby."

Generally, a clause followed by "when" takes the indicative, and a clause followed by "if" takes the subjunctive.

Mrs. Grammar Person knows exactly what your next question will be--it's one of her many talents. *You want to know how to use the subjunctive in the past tense.* Well, it's quite simple: to use the past subjunctive you need only remember: *had*, as *if* and *as though*.

The past subjunctive following *as if* or *as though* is used to indicate an unreal situation:

He was running *as if he were* being chased by aliens. (Let's hope not!)

She stared at me *as if* I were guilty. (I was framed!)

He talked about prison *as though* he had been there, himself. (Poseur!)

When we use the word *had* for the past subjunctive, the word *if* is understood, but not stated: *Had* he *known* about the rain, he wouldn't have gone to the concert. (We hope he enjoyed the concert, anyway.)

And now you've done it, you've learned the subjunctive! Mrs. Grammar Person congratulates you for mastering this difficult task so quickly. You are truly gifted grammarians, she says. As she sees the last of

you out with a heartfelt good-bye, she sighs and mur-
murs to herself, "Oh, how I *wish* I *were* younger."

A familiar voice behind her answers, "My dear, I
insist that you *take* that back."

Mrs. G.P. turns around and gives her friend a
smile. "But, Mr. Syntax, it's true! *Had* I *known* then
what I know now, just think what I could have accom-
plished!"

The gentleman takes both of her hands in his.
"You are the incomparable Mrs. Grammar Person and
I wouldn't change one thing about you. You are per-
fect just the way you are."

Our favorite grammarian squeezes his hand and
blushes, but says nothing. Something remarkable has
happened--for the first time in her life, Mrs. Grammar
Person cannot think of anything to say. Her words
have escaped, taking wing together for one joyful moment in time.

MRS. GRAMMAR PERSON TELLS A STORY

Fear not, Gentle Writer, Mrs. Grammar Person knows you've been working hard and is sure that you deserve a break. **To that end**, she has invited you to join her for tea and, **while** you rest up, she will tell you a story. Mrs. G.P. reminds us that all writing should tell a story and have a proper beginning, middle, and end. **But,** what is the glue that holds it all together? Mrs. G. P. is glad you asked that-- you talented grammarians! She will explain everything by and by, **but**, for now, she asks that you sit back, sip your Darjeeling and relax. Chocolate biscuit, anyone?

What kind of story would you like to hear? Our favorite grammarian has a wonderful idea, one that includes audience participation--a "build-your-own-story", if you like. **Once** she begins her tale, please pay attention and, **whenever** she pauses, you may fill in the blank from the choices she provides. Are you ready?

Once upon a time, there was a lonely *monkey/ orphan/ misshapen potato* making his way through the world as best he could. If anyone asked him, he would say that all he ever wanted in life was the chance to *marry a stockbroker/ judge a beauty contest/ compete on Jeopardy,* **but** he knew that this dream was out of reach, **so** he looked for a job instead. Nobody would give him a chance; they all said he was too *cantankerous/ sleep-deprived / mountaineering.* Frustrated, our hero turned to a life of crime and stole the king's favorite *grilled cheese sandwich/ talking parrot/ thesaurus.*

After that fateful day, our hero had to live on the run, **or** risk prison. **In the beginning**, he believed he needed only three things to survive. **First,** he needed his wits; **second**, his nerve; and **finally**, his *silly string/ pet ocelot / castanets.* **Also**, he could have used a friend. **In addition**, finding a hot meal seemed fairly urgent. **To be sure**, he wasn't used to such a hard life. **If** only he could find his favorite food: *figgy pudding/ milk moustache/ fried grasshoppers,* he knew he would feel better. **Equally important** was a place to rest his head, preferably somewhere without *bedbugs/ fleas/ a mint on the pillow.* **Finally**, after searching everywhere, our hero found the perfect job, one that provided food and shelter, friendship and camaraderie. **Above all**, it gave him a reason to get up in the morning. **In short**, it was the best job ever, **notwithstanding** the fact that he was covered with dirt and mud all the time. **In sum,** he was deliriously happy working as a *golf ball retriever/ gopher tracker/ dumpster diver* and was quite good at it. **As a result,** he eventually earned the king's pardon. It also helped that he returned the king's *grilled cheese sandwich/ talking parrot/ thesaurus.* **At last**, our tale is done.

More tea, anyone? Now that you have enjoyed our little story, it's time to talk about that glue, the handy words and phrases that connect our disparate thoughts and make them flow like a gentle brook through a verdant meadow, like caramel syrup over creamy custard, like--well, you get the picture. What are these useful links called? Anyone? Yes! They are **transition words** and are in **bold** above. While all of them are connectors, they serve different functions.

Some transitional words are used to indicate *similarity*. A few examples are: **in addition, likewise, furthermore, in the same way,** and **as well as.**

Contrastingly, some transitional words are used to indicate *dissimilarity or contradiction*. A few examples are: **in contrast, on the other hand, although, and yet,** and **however.**

Other transitional words are used for *emphasis*. A few examples are: **in fact, indeed, of course, truly,** and **even.**

And some transitional words are used for *place or position*. A few examples are: **above, adjacent to, beyond, below,** and **in front.**

Yet other transitional words are used to indicate *consequence*. A few examples are: **as a result, consequently, accordingly, thus,** and **therefore.**

Still other transitional words are used to indicate *time*. A few examples are: **after, during, earlier, to begin with,** and **next.**

Other transitional words are used to indicate *exemplifying*. A few examples are: **specifically, such as, namely, to illustrate**, and **for example.**

In this next group, transitional words are used to show the *priority* of the writer's thoughts. A few examples are: **above all, in the first place, of less/greater importance, moreover**, and **for one reason.**

In the following group, transitional words are used to provide *additional support*. A few examples are: a**dditionally**, **equally important, furthermore, in addition**, and **moreover.**

In our final group, transitional words **are** used to show conclusion. A few examples are: **in conclusion, in short, in summary, to conclude**, and **thus.**

Congratulations! You have mastered the concept of transitions--and without even trying. Look at Mrs. Grammar Person beaming with pride. But, don't go yet, please have another biscuit as Mrs. G.P. has one more thing to tell you and it is this: no matter what you write, be it a novel, a treatise, an essay, or a poem, you always have the same three goals: present the problem, work through the problem, resolve the problem. Once you've learned how to write a beginning, middle and an end, you'll be able to tell your own stories. And what could be better than that? Nothing-- except for tea with Mrs. Grammar Person, of course.

Fear not Gentle Writer, Mrs. Grammar Person has returned and she is delighted to bring you good news. It turns out that you are more talented than you knew. Yes, you are multilingual! You don't believe Mrs. G.P.? She would be happy to enlighten you. After all, it's what she lives for. Being the astute grammarians that you are you already know that countless English words derive from Latin, but did you know this?

If you like *sugar* in your *coffee*, play *chess*, understand *algebra*, and eat *candy* while sitting on your *sofa* reading a *magazine* and enjoying the fragrance of *lilac* and *jasmine*, then congratulations, you speak Arabic!

If you have ever been in a *hurricane* in *Florida*, eaten an *avocado* in *California*, or sipped a *daiquiri* in your *canoe*, while enjoying the *breeze* and carefully avoiding the *alligators* and *cockroaches*, then, congratulations, you speak Spanish!

If you graduated from *kindergarten* and like eating *hamburgers*, *frankfurters*, *noodles* and *strudel* all while sipping your wine *spritzer* and petting your *poodle* and your *dachshund*, then, congratulations, you speak German!

If you love reading *novels* (and who doesn't?) as you sit on your *patio* eating *pizza* and *broccoli*, listening to a *concert* featuring *cellos, oboes, pianos, trombones, violas, piccolos*, and *violins*, then, congratulations, you speak Italian! (And don't forget to deposit your *money* in the *bank*.)

If you have ever rowed your *dinghy* through the *jungle* in search of *cheetahs* while wearing your *pajamas* and drinking fruit *punch*, then, congratulations, you speak Hindi!

If you have ever ridden your *toboggan* in search of *raccoons, skunks, opossums, caribou, muskrats,* and *chipmunks* while munching on *pecans, persimmons,* and *squash*, then, congratulations, you speak the language of Native Americans!

If you have ever run the *gauntlet* on a *moped* on your way to a *smorgasbord* of *rutabagas* and *lingonberries* (and who hasn't?), then, congratulations, you speak Swedish!

If you have ever felt the urge to dance the *merengue*, the *mambo*, the *samba*, or the *tango* while sipping a *cola* and listening to the *jukebox* with your pet *zebra*, then, congratulations, you speak the languages of Africa!

Now, do you see how talented you are? But what about French, you ask? You are so clever, of course you speak French! Our beloved grammarian was saving the best for last, just for you, the *crème de la crème* and her *raison d'être*.

Mrs. G.P. has so *enjoyed* the *unique pleasure* of your company--it is hard to *imagine* how many *quests* you have undertaken, *adventures* you have been on, and *discoveries* you have made together. You have explored *pronunciation* and *grammar* through *poem* and *prose*; you have learned to use *reason*; you have mastered the *mystery* of the *apostrophe* and the *marvel* of the story. Now it is time to *celebrate* your *courage,* your *ambition*, and your *affinity* for language. Wouldn't you *agree?*

Therefore, your *gracious* host and favorite grammar person invites you to join her for a *feast* at her favorite *gourmet restaurant,* "The Bon Mot" where the pastry *chef* is a personal friend of hers. His *desserts* are *delicious!* Be sure to try the *orange marmalade biscuit* and the *cherry parfait* with *almond* and *licorice gelatin.* The *dinner* will be served *buffet*-style with plenty of meats like *bacon, beef* and *veal,* but, since Mrs. G.P. is a vegetarian, she will enjoy the *endive* with *mustard* dressing. Such an *abundance* of food, it is *absurd!* But, of course, it's not *quantity* that counts, it's *quality*.

Ah, here comes the pastry chef now, a man with a big moustache. It's clear to see that Mrs. G.P. *adores* him and that he also greatly *admires* her. Could it be? Is it possible? *Sacre bleu!* Mrs. Grammar Person has a *beau*--surely, you have guessed his name by now. Who knew that Mr. Syntax was French? From the French word *syntaxe,* to put together in order; it all makes sense now.

It is with deep *affection* that Mrs. G.P. must now bid *adieu* to all of you, her *brilliant protégés,* her *bons amis.* And, if you are ever in the neighborhood, she asks that you do stop by for tea. She always buys extra biscuits, just in case.

Dear reader,

We hope you enjoyed reading *Teatime With Mrs. Grammar Person*. Please take a moment to leave a review, even if it's a short one. Your opinion is important to us.

Discover more books by Barbara Venkataraman at https://www.nextchapter.pub/authors/barbara-venkataraman

Want to know when one of our books is free or discounted? Join the newsletter at http://eepurl.com/bqqB3H

Best regards,
Barbara Venkataraman and the Next Chapter Team

ABOUT THE AUTHOR

Award-winning author Barbara Venkataraman is an attorney in South Florida where she draws inspiration for her books from the daily headlines. She loves connecting with readers through her books and finds a particular kind of joy in a well-turned phrase. In addition to writing fiction, she co-authored *Accidental Activist: Justice for the Groveland Four* with her son Josh Venkataraman about his successful four-year quest to obtain posthumous pardons for The Groveland Four.

Teatime With Mrs. Grammar Person
ISBN: 978-4-86752-658-3
Mass Market

Published by
Next Chapter
1-60-20 Minami-Otsuka
170-0005 Toshima-Ku, Tokyo
+818035793528

5th August 2021

www.ingramcontent.com/pod-product-compliance
Lightning Source LLC
LaVergne TN
LVHW031241190726
843491LV00012B/3072

9 784867 526583